FLYOVER SEASONS

FLYOVER SEASONS

Flyover Seasons

Gene Stark

NORTH STAR PRESS OF ST. CLOUD, INC.
Saint Cloud, Minnesota

Copyright © 2011 Gene Stark

ISBN-13: 978-0-87839-555-2

All rights reserved.

First Edition, June 2011

Printed in the United States of America

Published by
North Star Press of St. Cloud, Inc.
P.O. Box 451
St. Cloud, Minnesota 56302

www.northstarpress.com

TABLE OF CONTENTS

I. GENERATIONS

1 Flyover Season	3
2 The Infrastructure	4
3 The Change	5
4 The March Snow	6
5 The Ice Eater	7
6 The Mock Spring	8
7 The Little Month	9
8 The Morning Break	10
9 The Greening	11
10 The Awakening	12
11 The Tilling Time	13
12 The Seed Season	14
13 The Straight Green Lines	15
14 The Country School	16

II. ACCELERATIONS

15 The Farmer	19
16 The Hill-Walkers	20
17 The Old Hand	21
18 The Long Days	22
19 The Tall Grass Days	23
20 The Red Moon	24
21 The Green Moment	25
22 The Dry-Landers	26
23 The Swap	27
24 The Summer	28

III. Culminations

25 The Shedding	31
26 The Harvest	32
27 The Coot	33
28 The Migration	34

IV. Hibernations

29 The Time of With-drawl	37
30 The Short Days	38
31 The January Moon	39
32 The Ice Storm	40
33 The Dormant	41

V. Determinations

34 The Common Ground	45
35 The Gravel Road	46
36 The Land	47
37 The Flyover	48

FLYOVER SEASONS

I

Generations

1. Flyover Season

A pattern emerges now
That I've watched and learned,
Seen the seasons turned
Knowing of the rhyme,
The marching time
The rhythm of the seasonal flow.
They come and go,
The seasons of the land.

2. The Infrastructure

The roads that wind us
Between moonlit lakes and dark hills,
Bind us tight to freeze and burn,
Right and wrong, straight or turn.
String us bead to bead
Past to future, hearsay to creed.
Roads that take us deep into the passion
Of the land,
Take us on trips unplanned.
Past generations piled deep into the earth,
Stacked one upon the next
And we perched atop.
Warmth of a new season has thawed our vision,
Clawed away the thatch of those defiled
And led us to our children's child.

3. The Change

It creeps in again,
The same feel of rain and snow,
Wind and bending trees.
Like it's crept and forced its way upon the land
For years before me.
Days of shrapnel-festered wounds,
Knew no difference in the way it re-froze
The March-softened fields.
Now, in techno-enhanced videos of the day,
The black-and-white films of winter's waning
Promise a season with a purpose;
Gaining, warming, permanent staining
Of the brown meadows.
How could we know, as kids,
That now the same arms of water, wind, and fire
Would embrace the land, as though nothing had changed.
Colors and beliefs have melded on the streets,
Yet here the shades are still distinctly
Unchanged as the cycle duplicates for time unmeasured.
That is the comfort in the dead-time,
The bottom line,
The rock beneath the muck of knowing,
How far we've come and how little we've gained.

4. The March Snow

Winter is not done with us yet.
New snow, wet and clinging to the roads.
But we hardly notice now, don't even mention it,
Go on our way, hardly pause;
Winter replacing thaws.
Dulled nails dig less deep than December's stinging talons.
New winter veils premature thoughts
Of water running days.
Patience in the muffling layer plays our minds.
Change is slow, reversals abound,
Repelled by frozen ground
Which shelters roots driven deep.
And now there are drifts to plow before we sleep
With Change's white protective layer,
As comes again, the March snow.

5. THE ICE EATER

The breath of Dixie
Banked off the Rockies:
The death of winter
Shears the prairie snow,
Moderating flow,
Expose the lifeless rubble
Of a season lost.
We are tossed and teased,
Made to believe
That short sleeves and seed hats will do.
Clean the hills to black and brown
Darken marsh ice down
To a liquid common denominator
Sucking frost from dead earth,
Consuming all that's hard and cold, and gray;
Stories told on winter nights
End now in the teeth of day.

6. The Mock Spring

Today is a frail spit of spring,
A day that clings for dear life to a southern breeze.
Surrounded by the gray fingers of March
It frees us for a moment to indulge.
We wonder ahead to days with no fear of their flight.
Solid days, long light;
Greening in the low corners of the field.
Days that yield progress and send us
To tasks undoable.
But today we perch upon a shaky, honeycombed,
Semblance of spring
Not yet ready to bring
Commitment from its frosty case.

7. The Little Month

The sun has had its way each day,
As the ever-earlier climb
Meets Holstein-colored hills.
More time to pester lingering snow,
Brief glimpse of warm times.
We'll pay, no doubt,
As vacillating fits, turn about our lives
And direct our days.
Pulled back and forth, ruled
By a fickle disc, ninety-three million miles away
We ponder length of days,
Three minutes more each time around
We're on the rebound now,
The hopeful tide, cycle turned.
Hang on and ride.

8. The Morning Break

Standing alone there,
White smoke circling, filtered
Through her long dark hair.
Thawing dregs of winter
Dripping on the backdoor walk,
No one to talk.
Pushed out to suck the life
From dwindling stocks,
Pushed to the edge of graying locks,
Nudged to the wind-at-your-back-breaks
Demanded by the corrected race,
She fades there now in the mist,
Stooped and kissed by the winds of change;
Swept from the pinnacle of glory
To the typing-pool of life.

9. The Greening

Last shreds of ice tinkle across the marshland,
Old reeds stand and bend,
Defend their last rites
As a newness creeps,
Seeps into the lowlands
And wedges into the hillsides.
Still no sign of leaves or flowers,
The sun empowers our daily climb,
We run to meet the unleashed warmth of day.
It splits into our soul, diminished by the cold winds
It hits us between the eyes of reality,
And coaxes us out.

10. The Awakening

Waking up to a black-and-blue sky,
The land and I, ready to till and take;
Black dirt awake for the hundredth time or so,
And I'm sure it's meant for me,
As some pioneer, hell-bent to claim it as his own
Stuck a shovel into the matted, tall-grass roots.
It gets in our boots and causes us to stand a bit taller,
To command the season.
Always a reason to stick our metal into
The back of the land.
So here I stand caught in the crack of time
Where earth and water join,
Blue and brown and black
Forced to hold the mindless cycle,
Continue to mold the fields
With diesel fuel and steel.

11. The Tilling Time

What are the patterns of these days?
Ever-lengthening rays of subtle green;
Less night, and sounds unheard a month ago.
We pattern our lives to flow
Ever-faster towards the sun,
Accelerated run to longest days.
Egrets wade where ice washed two weeks ago.
And still we know the patterns must prevail,
Must focus on the perfect days to plant the future.
Now we sow into earth, warmed to trigger newness,
Farmed again by temporary tenders,
To propagate the patterns of our days.

12. The Seed Season

Wild grass turning on an empty sky,
Ripe grain burning on a foreign sea.
Another seeding season
Caught between reason and red diesel fuel.
Corn profits turning in the corporate rain,
Farm kids burning in the urban sprawl.
Subsidized to mediocrity,
Mortgaged down the drain,
It gets hard to tell
Where wild grass meets the grain.

13. The Straight Green Lines

Straight green lines
Show our intersection with the land.
Monsanto planned
Our designs upon the earth.
We are trained, like the seeds we plant,
To fill the summer;
Strained to produce the volume required.
We are wired to the soil and shorted to the bank,
No one to thank but John Deere and the ghosts of prairie grass.
Only stacks of papers pass,
As we've become the government program of a generation
That's fed and clothed in the blood of a dream,
A thin stream of sweat and honesty,
Carrying the soiled cargo of a nation.

14. The Country School

School's out, taunting voices spread
To greening hills.
A silence fills, the teacher sighs;
A pile of papers, chalk dust hands.
Contentment in the smell
Of someone's rotting lunch.
The hunch-back floor and graying siding
Slowly finding oneness with the dust.
She knows she must retrieve the flag,
And walks between the crooked desks.
An opened door contests the rankness
Of the empty room.
Greening in the cracked steps that lead away
She gazes after loitering kids,
Bids them to the rolling land from where they came
And fades behind their long-forgotten names.

II

Accelerations

15. The Farmer

Seventy-five, still milking Holsteins
Twice a day.
"Someone's got to pay."
The banker called to say
"Happy birthday."
Free and clear,
Daddy had the land.
As kids we'd stand,
Look to the creek and beyond: blue skies,
See the future in Daddy's eyes.
The farmer's dream,
Take the cream, plow more black furrows,
Listen to the export quotas
And the bankers' stream of cash flow.
Rivers dried like the ink on the note.
And now we stay because we must,
A value quote, no one left to trust.

16. The Hill-Walkers

Shaggy, untethered beasts patrolled the plains,
Little remains of the raging swarms.
Sunset silhouettes the darkened outlines,
Stalking inclines and draws.
Movement imperceptible on thirsty grades
Trails made in circles on the land
I hear the patterned whisper in the leaves,
Water weaves its way to parched ground.
The untiring walkers, tied like leashed dogs
Take repetitious jogs around the pre-determined route.
Hill-walkers chest deep in the chosen grass,
They too will pass into the summer night.

17. The Old Hand

"Coffee, Black."
Red eyes, stooped back,
Tobacco juice in the corners of his lips,
Finger tips, cracked.
"Couple over-easies, ham."
No doubt, a business plan
In his barbwire office.
Day's break spent here,
Dusty boots appear to
Prop him up,
Hold his posture straight,
A little late to catch the curve of prosperity.
(If indeed it existed here)
Clear days have rusted him,
The years have busted him;
Spent the sagebrush inheritance
On old trucks and fence-posts.
The luck of this land
Rests on his broken frame
Things still the same, as ever.

18. The Long Days

The days slide their silvered fingers
Through the shades before the dawn.
We are drawn to wake before
The alarm sounds the day.
Short sleep to waking green;
One day seen in last year's brown,
Now leaping to the sun in emerald gown.
And so we are changed
Beyond the normal schedule of the days.
We are drawn up from sleepy winter ways
To feed upon the light,
Clawing deep into the softened earth,
Shunning sleep to shred the forging growth.
We and the prairie grasses alike
Fueled by generous sun
Step up a notch to run
Before the solstice passes.

19. The Tall Grass Days

Tall grass days,
Looking through a summer haze,
Quadrupled life ablaze.
Ease and complacency drawn
From midnight showers
And misty dawn.
Stop it now, freeze the season,
Keep us stuck in time to suck the marrow from the year;
Yet clear sunny days only march us
To the maze of leaner days.
But these are grasshopper times, paying little attention to
    the ants,
As the sun slants through the green leaves and waving grass.
We are caught for a moment in the lazy time.
Yet, we are snapped to the ever-looming reality,
Trapped in the current of the season,
To look in awe as we pass, swept on by tedious reason.

20. The Red Moon

Blood-light on the trees of a solstice night
Fireflies flash their unread code,
And we think we might
Stay out a bit longer.
Still a short sleeve breeze keeps us free
From a yellow-light-bulb-on-the-porch night.
A party night,
Kids scare each other and chase shadows,
Coyotes howl with bellies full of the year's young.
The sound of corn growing hung in the air.
And do we dare relax our grip,
Allow one moment for the fat to drip upon our lives,
For the code of the ages to unravel before our eyes
On the magic rise of one night's light?

21. The Green Moment

It's the fat time,
Zenith climb,
Green in its prime,
Sit on the porch and rhyme.
And we wonder when
Will it push over the top,
The wholesale greening stop
The holding pattern for a moment topped
By the spatter of a dusty raindrop.
A breath or two
The apex morning dew
Just as soon the porch is cleared,
A dusty raindrop smeared
To mud
And joined on the browning ride
The quickening slide
Past yellow flowers
And State Fair showers,
A wrinkling race
Come face to face with time.

22. The Dry-Landers

Some days nearly choke us
In the stubble-breath of a south wind.
Pinned to a crack
In a dusty field,
Skin peeled
From exposed ears.
The hazy day appears
To write our names on dusty dashboards.
Another day for corn
To wilt and dig deeper
As Dad listens
To the keeper of the secrets
On the weather channel.
Some march pivots around the hills,
Chased by dollar bills
And signed notes.
We dry-landers pray,
That somehow the mercy of this land
Will show up again.
Manifest in rain.
To cover our misdeeds:
Uncultivated weeds,
Late-planted beans,
Filthy screens that blacken kitchen floors.
We always look west
Where clouds might form,
Always the future is there,
The optimism that makes us take the yearly dare.

23. The Swap

Towers of foam to our south,
Rumbles and flashes, rain just missed.
Some farmers happy, others pissed.
Days built from steamy, still mists on mirror lakes,
The eye of summer takes our breath away.
Each day
The crops strain another inch,
Pushed even harder by now-shortening days.
And even Death plays games in bloomed-out summer's
        flowers;
Devours young broods in predatory fits.
But we can sit now and drink lemonade on the porch
After sweating the last ounce of wickedness from our pores,
Tempted once more, but not quite,
(Weakened by heat and vexed,)
To yearn for the inevitable swap
Of one madness for the next.

24. The Summer

A hole burned in the end of day,
Smooth and hot
Turned to fire and left to sink.
I think we've scorched too long.
Shimmering green days melded
To the haze of picking grain.
We're driven insane by plastic bats
And children in the park.
Embark me now upon
The ever-shortening river of the sun.
Lead me through the mega-days
Of seeking shade and a picnic basket lunch.
Take me to the Sunday brunch at church,
Help me search the memories of the day:
Hay clouds that leave so fast
And drive a naked sky into the sea of night.
Help me remember how fleeting this snapshot
Of the melted time, how quickly it erodes from sight.

III

Culminations

25. The Shedding

Divesting weeks of dropping leaves,
Cropping hayfields,
Subtle leaks
Of fleeting green.
We have seen
The fattest times, the wooly vines
Wrapped around the land.
Now we stand
To watch the fat plucked,
One field at a time,
To bare our hearts and tear apart
The summer's tedious coat,
Thinning now ahead of cold.
Lost migrants fly, flowers die
And naked soil unfolds
Before the frosty cleansing death.
How strange to shed the summer cloak
To welcome winter's breath.

26. The Harvest

Off the bottom step of the combine,
A star-specked night is mine.
I've chopped the last shreds of life
From the field,
Peeled the final layer of gold
From the land.
Now I stand in silence;
Done it again like a thousand neighbors
In a decade of years.
Laced with tears of salt and blood
I weep into the dirt of my fathers.
What have I heaped onto the pile
Of rotting grass,
And what will pass now into
The season of the blackened soil
To resurrect the sinews of tomorrow?

27. The Coot

I've never seen them fly in graceful vees, never seem them come or go
Never seen them sweep across the skies in the sun's last golden glow.
But huddled in their teeming flocks they appear one bright fall day,
Diving and feeding there, near the shore of Bottle Bay.
No one knows where they all come from, we've never seen them land,
But they dip and bob and splash a few yards from the sand.
Some say they feed on fish; wearing dark suits with hookish bills,
More likely though, their needs are fueled by some mysterious krill.
Coded signals fill their heads and drive their stay here on our lake,
While sinister and universal plans they seem to make.
They're a pure and solid race, never mix with ducks or geese,
Dark hordes, they wait for some telepathic sign to summon their release.
There's more than meets the eye, I've found as I've watched them through the years
I've mounded up some troubling thoughts and unexplainable fears.
Long nights and fall lake mists, must hide unearthly plans and deeds
As innocent-looking water birds mill among the reeds.
I opened up my door on a cold and frosty night,
To the extra-terrestrial glow of the eerie northern lights.
I know strange things can happen under the Aurora's cold display
But the next morning as I passed the lake I saw the empty bay.
Not a trace of birds or feathers near the reed and sandy strip
I knew at once that the troops had been, beamed up by the mother ship.

28. The Migration

In the Minni-apple on a pure and cloudless eve,
Red and yellow light reflects the towers as they leave.
There are many living on the brink of city lights and back
    woods nights,
Edge-people who charge and retreat, who daily keep the
    rhythm rites.
Two-world beings caught between; never quite there,
Stretched and dried by mingled autumn air.
Drawn by childhood memories under clouds by clear
    streams,
Yet attracted by the lights like moths they fly to catch their
    dreams.
Park-raised geese struggle into flight,
To visit ancient fields beyond the city light.
Most return in patterns much the same,
A few stay lost from where they came.

IV

Hibernations

29. THE TIME OF WITH-DRAWL

Tree-laced sunsets come early now.
Piercing horizontal rays
Glance off the deeply piled misery on the fields.
Endless scraping yields but frozen bits of life
To frost-encrusted whitetails.
Pheasants scratch for hours now
To get what last month was free.
Chain-marked tracks lead to drifted-over bales,
Stubble marks the emptied spots.
Profitless taking now,
Living on the interest of the season past.

30. The Short Days

Frozen, carbon copy days
Flutter through the icy haze of deepest repetition.
It has us by the throat,
Pinned to solstice walls against our backs
Of gray and white and black.
Sun limps the perimeter of red-twigs and peeling bark,
Dives the shortest mark,
Then leaves again as all life that can, has done.
Only we burrowers are left
To scuttle through the carcasses, yet unpicked,
Mingling with and drawn, to killers and scavengers,
Piecing together the bones of dawn.

31. The January Moon

The January moon seldom fails
To lead my gaze from sky to diamond snow.
It seldom fails to make me know
The shadows hidden deep at other times.
The January moon seldom fails to paint
The white/gray frosting on snowshoe trails
It seldom fails to light the way
Of cold stalkers and silent flight.
It seldom fails to expose the night,
Bare and naked sight,
Of reddened snow at end of frozen tracks.
The January moon seldom fails
To taunt of beauty viewed from warm window rails
And seldom fails to smile on stiffened scenes.
Never fails to bury its glowing flight
Into the earth, made one notch colder by its light.

32. The Ice Storm

They die there now.
Perish by the thousands,
Life only a fraction of an inch away,
Yet encased by winter's indecision.
The tall grass groans.
Pestered by a breeze,
Cracking at the knees.
Now splayed and useless.
The sun-after, would have it all in diamonds,
Try to gild our sorrows in supernatural brightness,
But we know the cold and lifeless forms
That bow forever under translucent veils.

33. The Dormant

What rests there,
Beneath the mantle of the stiffened ground?
What future beauties
Stopped and suspended under ever-shortening days?
Crouched there,
Shielded by the white Kevlar on the land
Waiting for the sun to call again.
Take a lesson from the land.
Immobilized plans,
Buried in our minds,
Stopped and sealed for a time
We wait, the earth and I,
For great things to be released.
Dormant now, we'll break the crust
And burst into a brightening time.

V

Determinations

34. The Common Ground

"Name's Nels," I shook hands with a rusty pliers.
Looked me straight in the eye, not the look of a liar.
No lies either in the greasy jeans or shitty shoes,
He'd worked this place, paid his dues.
"Mostly me and the boy milk, and hay, put in the crops."
I looked around and saw few modern props.
A curtain rustled in the graying place
Sun slipped behind the windbreak's face.
We talked of the crops, the markets, the land,
Politicians we fired, elected, and damned.
We plotted the economy, propped up the buck,
Figured how to save fuel in the old Chevy truck.
We talked until dark, we shared brilliance and insight,
We solved most world problems that night.
As he creaked up those rotting stairs to sleep
I headed home in my old rusty Jeep.

35. The Gravel Road

Wild meandering chameleon,
Styled to suite the season.
Freshly bladed now,
Spring's soft plow sets your peaceable disposition.
We need your changing ride,
Direction tried and true
Yet each month we're kept to wonder
What surprises to expect of you.
Take us to our little piece of heaven in the hills,
Feed us summer dust and grit
That fills our nose and eyes;
Hard ride, but fast.
Slow us in your foggy, fall-ish nights:
Picking our way from fence corner to neighbors' hazy lights.
Hold us on your icy crown,
Winter trips to town,
White knuckles steering hard and true.
Just let us pass
As frost releases mire,
Clutching low-spots sucking at our tires.
We follow your fickle moods
As change broods
In this land sometimes forsaken.
You will always take us here,
Because we are always ripe to be taken.

36. The Land

What is this place that holds us?
Forgives us in the winds of change,
Folds us into summer green,
Keeps us warm in winter lean.
What song she puts into our head,
Of fire and ice she sings.
On egret wings, undulating in the breeze
Takes us to our knees
On shores of pulsing grass.
We wait to sail upon the land
Testing waters yet unmanned,
She sings and pilots us
Past the lost, in summer hail and winter wind.
Past those who sinned
By signing off their temporary gift,
But now she lifts us beyond the lifetime lease
To see she's there even after we might cease.

37. The Fly-over

Silver wings and contrails paint names
Across our sky,
They fly from coast to coast.
Quick gaze at our patchwork land
Once white and black, then green and blue
Glide through, enroute.
Little glance from laptop light
To silent scenes below
They come and in a cutting shard they go.
Yet our fathers left us here
To work the space and
Pump the bounty to the coasts,
And keep the secrets of the land.
We stand, look up, wonder where they go,
Thank God they mostly do.